海倫·凱勒

Heroes and Role Models | Non-Fiction Series

Copyright © 2022 by Level Learning, INC. and Washington Yu Ying PCS™
Original and Edited Text Copyright © 2022 by Washington Yu Ying PCS™

All rights reserved. No part of this book in whole or part may be reproduced without written permission from the publisher.

Published by Level Learning, INC.

Content Contributors:
Washington Yu Ying PCS™
Level Learning - Ya-Ching Chang

Illustrations by: Josh Taira

Leveling classification based on Level Learning standard.
For full description, visit www.levellearning.com

ISBN 978-1-64040-040-5
Traditional Chinese Edition

About Level Learning:
Level Learning provides a literacy focused curriculum specifically designed for K-12 Chinese as a Second Language classrooms. Our program offers 20 levels of specific and detailed objectives, leveled texts and passages, mastery-based online assessment, and analytics to enable data-driven instruction. Level Learning reading curriculum for both literature and informational text emphasize grammar and comprehension skills to help teachers develop confident and independent Chinese language readers. The non-fiction series of books are specifically designed to support our informational text course based on multiple national standards. To learn more about our entire offering, visit www.levellearning.com.

About Washington Yu Ying PCS™:
Washington Yu Ying PCS is a Mandarin English dual language immersion International Baccalaureate (IB) World school. Yu Ying's mission is to inspire and prepare young people to create a better world by challenging them to reach their full potential in a nurturing Chinese/English educational environment. Yu Ying's comprehensive IB, dual immersion curriculum equips students with global competencies for success in the real world. As a leader in immersion education, Yu Ying is determined to advance Chinese language programs and global citizenry education by helping other schools create and strengthen their Chinese programs. For more information, email: products@washingtonyuying.org

海倫·凱勒出生於1880年。她是一位著名的美國作家。

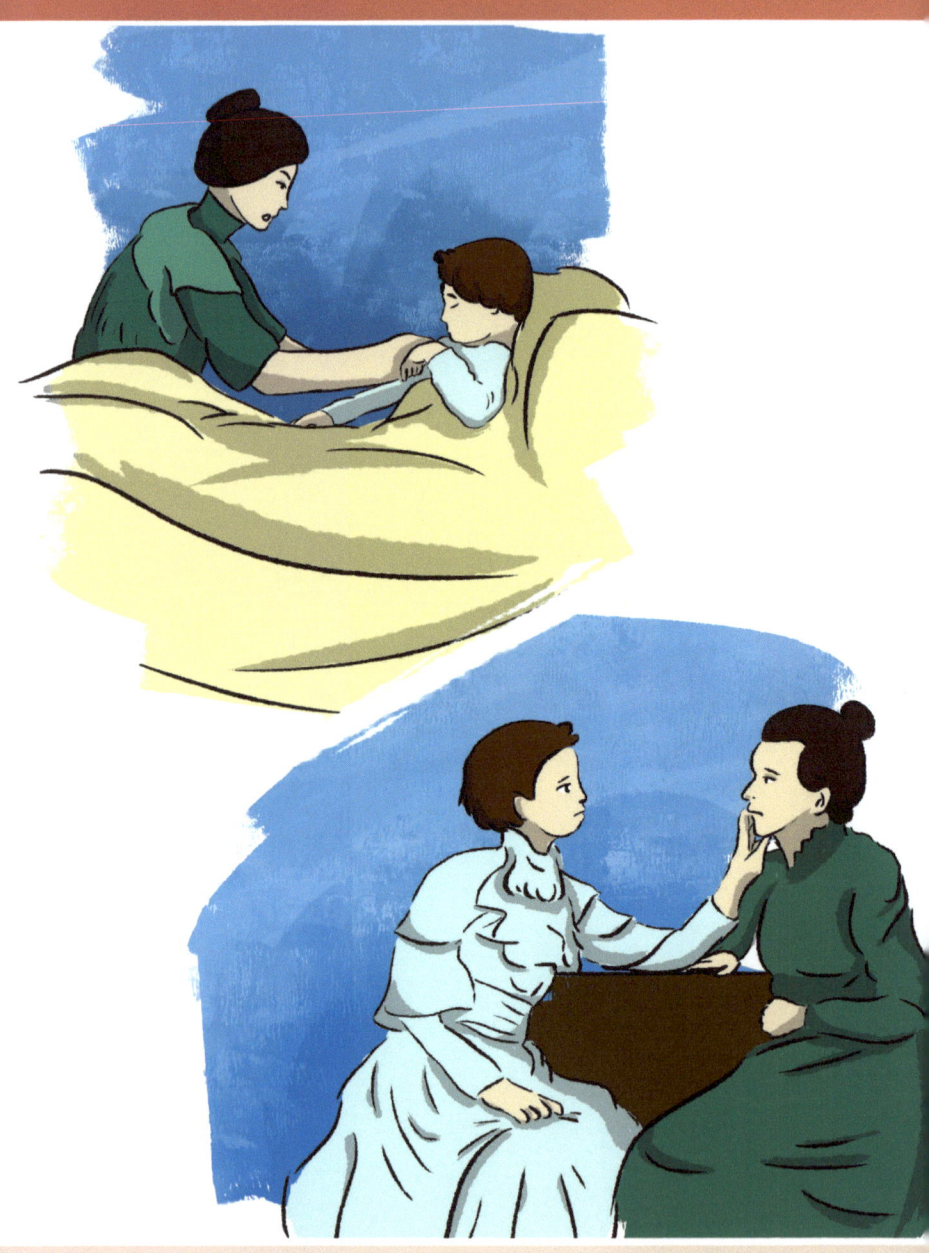

海倫·凱勒小時候生了一場病。這場病讓她失去了聽力和視力。因為聽不見也看不到，所以她也不會說話。

長大以後,她知道自己和別人不一樣,這讓她常常感到生氣和傷心。別人可以讀書,但是她不能讀書。別人可以說話,但是她不能說話。

別人的世界是彩色的,海倫·凱勒的世界卻是一個黑色的、沒有聲音的地方。

在海倫·凱勒七歲的時候，她的爸爸媽媽幫她找了一位老師。這位老師用了許多方法教她，可是海倫·凱勒都不明白。

有一天,這個老師帶她出去玩水。老師把水灑到她的頭上、臉上和手上,然後重複地把「水」這個字寫在她的手上。這時候,海倫·凱勒知道了,原來老師寫在她手上的字,就是「水」。

在老師的幫助下,海倫·凱勒學會了用盲人點字法來讀書,也學會了說話。雖然她花了比別人更多的時間學習,但是她感到很開心。她覺得這個世界變成彩色的了!

長大以後,海倫·凱勒成為一位著名的作家。除了寫書,她還到處演講,因為她想要分享自己的故事來鼓勵別人。

海倫‧凱勒讓大家知道，雖然盲人看不見，但是他們和正常人一樣。盲人可以讀書，盲人也可以做許多事情。

Glossary

	Pinyin	English Definition
著名	zhù míng	famous
作家	zuò jiā	writer
病	bìng	sickness
失去	shī qù	to lose
聽力	tīng lì	hearing
視力	shì lì	vision, sight
世界	shì jiè	world
彩色	căi sè	color
聲音	shēng yīn	sound
方法	fāng fă	method, way
明白	míng bai	to understand
灑	să	to sprinkle, to spray
重複	chóng fù	to repeat
原來	yuán lái	turned out to be
盲人	máng rén	blind people

	Pinyin	English Definition
點字法	diǎn zì fǎ	Braille method
到處	dào chù	everywhere
演講	yǎn jiǎng	to give speeches
分享	fēn xiǎng	to share
鼓勵	gǔ lì	to encourage
正常	zhèng cháng	normal